SUPER BRAIN
BAFFLERS

Robert Steinwachs

D1280115

PUZZLE
WRIGHT
PRESS

An imprint of Sterling
Publishing Co., Inc.
www.puzzlewright.com

Puzzlewright Press and the distinctive Puzzlewright Press logo
are trademarks of Sterling Publishing Co., Inc.

Edited by Francis Heaney
Illustrations by Jeff Moores

2 4 6 8 10 9 7 5 3

Published by Sterling Publishing Co., Inc.
387 Park Avenue South, New York, NY 10016
© 2009 by Robert Steinwachs
Distributed in Canada by Sterling Publishing
c/o Canadian Manda Group, 165 Dufferin Street
Toronto, Ontario, Canada M6K 3H6
Distributed in the United Kingdom by GMC Distribution Services
Castle Place, 166 High Street, Lewes, East Sussex, England BN7 1XU
Distributed in Australia by Capricorn Link (Australia) Pty. Ltd.
P.O. Box 704, Windsor, NSW 2756, Australia

Manufactured in the United States of America
All rights reserved

Sterling ISBN 978-1-4027-4643-7

For information about custom editions, special sales, premium and
corporate purchases, please contact Sterling Special Sales
Department at 800-805-5489 or specialsales@sterlingpublishing.com.

Contents

Acknowledgments

Special thanks to Ken Hughes, Louise Stark, Marie Steinwachs, Chris Steinwachs, George Cummings, Edward Padelford, Frank Twist, Foch Mckee, and Frank Yohn.

INTRODUCTION

L iving up to the standard set by the popular first edition of *Brain Bafflers* was a challenge, but we hope you'll agree we've succeeded with this follow-up. The book begins with a chapter of fascinating facts about the world, presented in puzzle form. We then offer varied math problems, from comparatively simple to more complex and difficult. The word and logic chapters likewise are wide-ranging and speckled with a few items on the lighter side to hold attention and interest throughout. Sometimes whether a puzzle is a math puzzle, a logic puzzle, or a word puzzle is a fuzzy question—some puzzles have elements of all three!—so be prepared for anything. You'll also find your memory tested (or your ability to listen to anecdotes from your grandparents' era) in chapter 6, and have the opportunity to impress or confuse your friends with some magic and "impossible" parlor tricks.

We hope this book provides our readers with as much fun solving the problems as we have had in presenting them.

—Robert Steinwachs

Chapter 1
The World We Live In

"The world is a beautiful book, but of little use to him who cannot read it." —Italian dramatist Carlo Goldoni

1. Nations of the World
There are approximately 200 countries in the world. Can you list 25 that each begin with a different letter of the alphabet? (There is no country that begins with X.) Getting 20 or more is excellent.

2. Incredible!
What remarkable thing did Ben Lecomte do in 1998?

3. Oldest Thing Alive?
Currently, what is considered to be the oldest living thing in the world?

4. Past the Expiration Date
What is the oldest known man-made alcoholic beverage?

5. Better Make That an Extra Large
What is the world's most popular drink (other than water)?
Is it beer? Milk? Coffee? Tea? Wine? Or soda?

6. Including You and Me
Name three things that everything in the universe is doing at all times.

7. Fish Story
The largest fish ever caught was landed at Knight's Key, Florida, in June 1912. Can you guess its weight within 1,000 pounds, and its length within 3 feet? (Remember, a whale is a mammal, not a fish.)

8. Let's Shrink the Sun
The sun is approximately 800,000 miles in diameter. If we could reduce its diameter to 9 feet (2.74 meters), what would you estimate the following sizes and distances to be in proportion?

    1) Size of Earth
    2) Size of Mars
    3) Distance from Earth to the Sun
    4) Distance from Earth to the Moon
    5) Distance from the Sun to the nearest star

9. The Birth of Broadcasting
What year was the first human voice broadcast over the radio waves?

10. City Dwellers
What five cities in the world have the largest populations? The average person can name only two of them correctly.

11. Drink Up
Is it possible to drink liquids while hanging upside down?

12. Mystery Destination
The distances below have all been measured from a famous landmark. What is it and where is it located?

From Tokyo, Japan: 6,052 miles (9,739 km)
From Cairo, Egypt: 2,001 miles (3,220 km)
From Fairbanks, Alaska: 4,432 miles (7,133 km)
From Oslo, Norway: 836 miles (1,345 km)
From Honolulu, Hawaii: 7,449 miles (11,987 km)
From London, England: 213 miles (1,343 km)

13. Capital Cities
Without any assistance, can you name the capital cities of these 34 countries? The average person can name only 7 of them correctly.

Argentina	Ireland
Australia	Italy
Austria	Japan
Bosnia	Liechtenstein
Brazil	Mexico
Belgium	Netherlands
Canada	Norway
China	Philippines
Cuba	Poland
Denmark	Russia
Egypt	Singapore
Ethiopia	Sweden
Finland	Switzerland
France	United Kingdom
Germany	United States
Greece	Venezuela
India	Vietnam

14. Hole to China

Many children have tried to "dig a hole to China" in their backyard (although usually they give up after making it down a few feet). If it were possible to drill a hole straight through the center of the earth to the opposite side, starting from anywhere in the U.S., would China be at the other end?

15. Answer When Ready

It is not liquid, gas, or solid. It is not animal, plant, or mineral. It is transparent, but can be seen from a distance, is always in motion, has no gender, but reproduces itself. It can be man's best friend or worst enemy. What is it?

16. Silent and Unseen

What are invisible but will penetrate a solid concrete wall and still be effective?

17. Span-tastic!

Where is the highest bridge in the world?

18. Extremes
Where were the hottest and the coldest temperatures ever recorded on earth?

19. Not So Tough
What did Alexander the Great, Julius Caesar, Genghis Khan, Napoleon, Mussolini, and Hitler have in common, besides tyranny and a thirst for world domination?

20. What Time Is It?
It is 12 noon on a Monday in Floral City, Florida. Can you figure out what the time would be in these other cities?

Floral City, Florida, U.S.	12 noon Monday
Buenos Aires, Argentina	_____
Denver, Colorado, U.S.	_____
Tokyo, Japan	_____
Siena, Italy	_____
Moscow, Russia	_____
Jefferson City, Missouri, U.S.	_____
Hong Kong, China	_____
Sydney, Australia	_____
Stockton, California, U.S.	_____
Wexford, Ireland	_____
Bangalore, India	_____

3 A.M. Monday	6 P.M. Monday
10 A.M. Monday	8 P.M. Monday
11 A.M. Monday	10 P.M. Monday
1 P.M. Monday	1 A.M. Tuesday
5 P.M. Monday	2 A.M. Tuesday
	3 A.M. Tuesday

21. High Rise
Where are the four tallest buildings in the world?

22. Eight Is Enough?
What letter should come next in this sequence? Does the sequence continue any further?

M, V, E, M, J, S, U, __

23. Not Out of the Woods Yet
Within ten feet, how tall is the tallest tree in the world, and where is it located?

24. Around the World
An airplane leaves London, England, which is located at 51 degrees latitude. If the plane circles the globe along that degree of latitude, it would fly over nine countries. How many of these nine countries can you name?

25. Between the Oceans
In America, the Atlantic Ocean is to the east and the Pacific Ocean is on the west. However, in one place on the continent it is just the opposite—the Atlantic is on the western shore and the Pacific is on the eastern coast. How can this be, and where is this place?

26. Let's Travel
Can you unscramble these anagrammed names of nations of the world? (Note that two of the nations' names are two-word phrases.)

CHAIN	SERIAL	UNSAD
LAITY	REGALIA	MEG RYAN
PLANE	BRAISE	KRAMDEN
REIGN	ALSO	SUMERIAN
TANGO	PURE	ESTIMATOR
TEARIER	RAIN	ROMANIANS

27. Moving In

The percentage of undeveloped land in Africa is a surprising figure. What would you estimate it to be?

28. Thank You

All the expressions below say thanks in various languages. Can you match the words with their place of origin?

1) Grazie	a) France
2) Danke	b) Spain
3) Dziekuje	c) Russia
4) Tak	d) Hawaii
5) Merci	e) Mongolia
6) Arigato	f) Netherlands
7) Gracias	g) Liberia
8) Bedankt	h) Japan
9) Spasibo	i) Italy
10) Bayarlalaa	j) Poland
11) Thank you	k) Germany
12) Mahalo	l) Denmark

29. Move Over
What rare trait is shared by the countries Egypt, Russia, Kazakhstan, and Turkey?

30. A Trip to the Winery
On a recent European trip, we wished to visit a local winery about 10 miles (16 km) from our village. Hans from Germany, Paulo from Italy, and Pierre from France accompanied us. After I drove a couple miles, Hans instructed me to "fahren Sie nach links," which I did, and traveled 3.2 kilometers. Then Paulo suggested that we "girare a sinistra." I did, and drove another 2 miles before taking Pierre's advice to "tourner à gauche." After 1.6 kilometers we thought we must be close, so I slowed down for the next mile to keep an eye out. How far from the winery were we after that?

31. Good Friends
What two countries have the longest border between them, and have always been peaceful neighbors?

32. Older Than a Buzzard
Buzzards (also known as vultures) are found in almost every country. It is truly amazing that they live on decayed foods and dead animals, can travel for long hours or distances while searching for food, and still have a lifespan of 40 years. Only three birds have a longer life expectancy. Can you name them?

33. Drive On
Where is the longest road in the world?

34. Almost the Most
What is the second most populated continent in the world?

35. Seafood Diners
What country consumes the most seafood per capita?

36. Hole Notes
Where on Earth is the deepest hole dug by human hands?
How about the deepest hole in the world? And how deep
do you think they both are?

Chapter 2
Fun With Numbers

"I don't believe in mathematics" —Albert Einstein

37. Astronomical?
If you multiplied 2 by 2 one hundred times, what would the answer be?

38. The Flagpole
A flagpole is 1/3 underground. A man paints 1/2 of its total length, but because his ladder is too short, he is unable to reach the top 4 feet of the pole. What is the total length of the flagpole?

39. Highway Travelers
The Alaska Highway is a road that extends 1,500 miles from Dawson Creek, British Columbia, to Fairbanks, Alaska. Bill left Dawson Creek by car on a Monday at 8 A.M. and Bob left Fairbanks by car at the same time. Each drove only eight hours a day. Bill averaged 55 mph the first day, 45 mph the second day, and 50 mph after that. Bob averaged 50 mph the entire trip. Which driver was closest to Fairbanks and by how much when Bob passed Bill on the highway?

40. Half Fun!
What number is .5 more than .5 of .5 of .5 of 500?

41. Big Business
Nathan bought a fishing rod for $2. He sold it to a friend for $3, bought it back for $4, and sold it for $5. Did he make a profit or lose money on the transactions?

42. Sitting Ducks
If seven ducks lay seven eggs in seven days, how long would it take for three ducks to lay three eggs at the same rate? How long for fifteen ducks to lay fifteen eggs?

43. Clock Watcher
Leave six adjacent numbers on the face of a clock intact, and rearrange the other six numbers so that the sum of every pair of numbers directly opposite each other is a prime. (Prime numbers are those not evenly divisible by any whole numbers besides themselves and 1—that is, 2, 3, 5, 7, 11, 13, 17, 19, and so on.)

44. Over and Under
What number is twice as much below 20 as 7 is above 4?

45. Dividing It Up
Megan, Maggie, and Lauren wish to buy a golf cart that costs $6,250. Megan, who is the oldest, offers to pay four times as much as Maggie, who is the youngest. Lauren says she will pay 1/4 of what the others paid together. How much did each pay for the cart?

46. No Adding

For the following challenges, you may use any mathematical symbols except addition signs: −, ×, ÷, !, decimals, parentheses, and exponents are all legal. (Subtracting a negative number is not allowed.)

1) Use eight 1s to equal 100.
2) Use eight 2s to equal 11.
3) Use five 3s to equal 33.
4) Use seven 4s to equal 44.
5) Use six 5s to equal 87.
6) Use seven 6s to equal 333.
7) Use eight 7s to equal 27.
8) Use seven 8s to equal 800.
9) Use eleven 9s to equal 99.

47. Ignorance of the Lawn Is No Excuse

A lawn measures 100 feet by 100 feet. The mower will cut a three-foot-wide swath. The owner cuts the lawn in a spiral from the outer edge to the center, taking a short break after each lap. After which lap is the job of mowing the lawn closest to being half finished?

48. I Think That I Shall Never See ...

Tom planted a 3-foot-tall cedar tree in his front yard. During the ninth year, it grew 10% more than its height at the end of the eighth year. Given that the annual increase in height was the same every time, how much did the tree grow each year?

49. Traveler's Check

$$A \times LONG = TRIP$$

Replace the letters with the numbers 1 to 9, using each number only once, to make the equation correct.

50. Seating the Guests
How many different ways can 12 people sit at a table? (Rotations and reflections are considered to be different.)

51. Cops and Robbers
Three men robbed the Floral City National Bank. To avoid drawing attention by exceeding speed limits they fled at a speed of 45 miles per hour. Sheriff's deputies followed 10 minutes later, pursuing at 60 miles per hour. After 20 minutes the police assumed that they had lost the robbers and gave up the search. How many more miles would they have had to drive to catch up with the fleeing car?

52. Dividing the Loot
The three men who robbed the Floral City bank fled with the money and were able to outrun the police. When they split the loot, the leader took one half plus $1,000 for doing the planning. The second man got half as much as the leader. That left $4,000 for the third man who drove the getaway car. How much money did they steal from the bank?

53. Missing Number
A mystery operation has been performed on the first two numbers in each equation to get the third number. Can you figure out what number completes the last equation?

$$15 \star 12 = 11$$
$$9 \star 22 = 14$$
$$33 \star 10 = \underline{\quad}$$

54. Computerization
A family decided to pool their money to purchase a computer for $1,125. Lauren contributed $10 less than her sister Maggie, and their father paid the balance with $860 more than Lauren. How much did each pay?

55. Cash Customer

Mr. Jones entered a store and chose a bottle of wine that cost $5. He wanted to pay with a $50 bill but Mr. Smith, the shopkeeper, did not have change, so Smith took it to the bakery next door to break into smaller bills. The shopkeeper was then able to give $45 change to Jones, who left with the bottle of wine. Soon after, the baker returned with the $50 bill and showed that it was counterfeit. Smith had to give him $50 for it. What was the total loss for the store?

56. Drive to the Airport

While driving to the airport nearest me, I maintain a fairly constant speed. If I decreased that average speed by 10 miles per hour, the trip would take me 30 minutes longer. If I increased the usual speed by 10 miles per hour, I would arrive 20 minutes earlier. How far is the airport from my home and what is my usual speed to drive there?

57. Plus and Minus

Using only plus and minus signs, make the equation below correct.

$$0 \quad 1 \quad 2 \quad 3 \quad 4 \quad 5 \quad 6 \quad 7 \quad 8 \quad 9 = 1$$

58. Square Deal

Using the numbers 1 to 16 once each (with four numbers already placed), fill in the empty squares so the horizontal, vertical, and two main diagonal lines all add up to the same total of 34.

		14	
12			
		11	
			16

59. Good Hunting

Two brothers went hunting separately, one accompanied by the family dog. After a while they saw one another, a half mile apart. They started walking toward each other at the rate of 2.5 miles per hour. The dog saw the second brother, ran to meet him, returned to the first brother, and went back and forth until they met. The dog runs nine miles an hour. How far did he run before the brothers met?

60. Football Practice

A father was teaching his 10-year-old son how to throw and catch a football. Each time he threw it he stepped back 3 feet. After the ball had been thrown back and forth for a total distance of 195 feet, the boy missed. How many times was the ball thrown back and forth? What was the length of the last throw?

61. Those Mighty Nines

Using addition, subtraction, multiplication, divison, and parentheses, can you create 5 different equations for which five 9s total 10?

62. Buying Rope

A man went into a store and ordered a piece of rope, giving the length in feet and inches. The clerk erred by listing the feet in inches, and the inches in feet. The result was that when the rope was delivered, it was only 30% of what the man ordered. How much rope did the man originally order?

63. Division of Labor
What is unusual about the number 2,520?

64. Quick, What's the Answer?
What is half of 2 + 2?

65. Chicken Shopping
Farmer Pete sent his son to town to buy some chickens, giving him $100 to buy 100 chickens. Hens were selling for $5, roosters for $2, and chicks were priced at 2 for $1. The boy was hungry and bought a $2 hamburger and was still able to buy exactly 100 chickens with the $98 he had left, with no money left over. How many of each kind did he buy?

66. Clearance Sale
A fabric store had six rolls of a discontinued fabric. The rolls measured 30 meters, 32 meters, 36 meters, 38 meters, 40 meters, and 62 meters. The store manager offered the six rolls at half price. Two rolls sold on the first day of the sale, and the next day three more rolls were sold. Those three rolls contained exactly twice as much fabric as the two rolls sold on the previous day. How long was the roll that was left?

67. Eight Training
All the numbers below are divisible by 8 except one. Without using the long process of dividing each number can you determine which of them is the misfit? There is a quick method.

$$462,344,984,160$$
$$102,677,981,804$$
$$399,421,566,328$$
$$133,030,348,864$$

68. Four You Alone

Build the numbers from 1 to 10 using only four 4s for each number. (For example, 44 ÷ 44 = 1.) You may use the mathematical symbols +, −, ×, ÷, !, decimals, and parentheses.

69. Cookie Time

Grandma made cookies and gave a third of them to one of her grandchildren. Then she gave one-fourth to another, one-fifth to the third, one-sixth to the youngest, and had 6 cookies left. How many did she bake?

70. Sharing the Profits

The owner of a small restaurant had a plan whereby a percentage of the profits was shared with the employees. The percentage last year amounted to $7,920. The cook got $302 more than the waitress, $882 more than the busboy, and $960 more than the dishwasher, which accounts for all the employees. How much did each receive?

71. Words From Numbers

10	6	1	7	4
6	8	12	3	9
1	12	1	9	3
7	3	9	11	3
4	9	3	3	6

10	1	6	1	2
1	1	1	2	5
6	1	10	5	7
1	2	5	7	4
2	5	7	4	13

Replace the numbers with letters of the alphabet. The words formed will read both across and down.

1 = A or B   2 = C or D   3 = E or F   4 = G or H
5 = I or J   6 = K or L   7 = M or N   8 = O or P
9 = Q or R   10 = S or T   11= U or V   12 = W or X
13 = Y or Z

72. The Calculating Jogger

A man jogging on a railroad bridge knows it will take three minutes for him to get across. He is one-fourth of the way across when he hears the whistle of a train coming from behind him. He knows the location of the crossing where the train signals, the speed of the train, and that it would take one minute for the train to reach the bridge. He realizes that by continuing to walk forward, he would be 15 seconds from the end of the bridge when the train reached him. However, he determines he has just enough time to return to the beginning of the bridge to get off before the train reaches it. His jogging speed is 8 miles per hour. How fast is the train coming?

73. The Race

Katie and Rachel are racing against each other. Both run at the same pace and walk at half their running speed. If Katie covered half of the distance running and the other half walking, and Rachel ran half of the time and walked the other half, who would win the race?

74. Squared Numbers
Three numbers squared total 139. Six numbers squared total 139. What are the numbers in each case? (The numbers within each set are different, but may repeat between sets.)

75. Bus Riders
The city bus left the terminal with both men and women passengers. At the first stop, one-third of the women got off and were replaced by the same number of men. At the next stop one-third of the men got off and were replaced by as many women. Now two more women than men were on the bus, and there were as many men as there were women originally. How many men and women were on the bus when it left the terminal?

76. Presents of Mind
An eccentric grandfather wants to give some money to his three grandsons. He places the money in envelopes in the following manner and seals them:

> 8 red envelopes each containing $5
> 8 blue envelopes each containing $3
> 8 green envelopes each containing $1

He wants to divide the sealed envelopes among his three grandsons so they will each receive the same amount of money, each get the same number of envelopes, and each get at least one envelope of each color. How can he distribute the envelopes to accomplish this?

77. Exchanging Change
Bill has 20 coins consisting of dimes and quarters. If the number of dimes and the number of quarters were reversed, he would have 90 cents more. How many of each kind of coin does he have?

78. Driving to Work

I drive an average of 40 miles per hour to get to work on time. One morning I had delays and at the halfway point realized that it had taken me twice as long as usual to get there. How much faster must I drive to make up the time?

79. Weight Watcher

Joe weighs 115 pounds more than his sister, Sue. Their combined weight is 135 pounds. How much does each weigh?

80. Halves and Quarters

What is 25 more than $1/2$ of $1/4$ of $1/2$ of $1/4$ of 24,000?

81. Hours of Fun

Use the numbers 1, 4, 5, and 6 in two equations, each of which totals 24. Use only those four numbers, and use each number only once. You may only add, subtract, multiply, and divide, and use parentheses. Digits may not be combined to make larger numbers (like making 15 out of the 1 and 5).

82. Math Teaser

Use the numbers 0 to 8 to fill in the blank spaces in the grid below, such that the rows and columns equal the totals given. (Perform the operations in order from left to right or top to bottom.)

0 1 2 3 4 5 6 7 8

	+		+		= 9
×	■	×	■	−	
	÷		×		= 10
÷	■	+	■	÷	
	×		−		= 31
= 3		= 8		= 2	

83. Three Ways

A mother has two boxes of candy to be divided equally among three boys. The pieces in each box are not evenly divisible by three but combining the boxes will make it possible. One box has seven more pieces than the other. Together, both hold over 100 pieces. What is the smallest amount of candy each box could possibly hold?

84. Test Yourself
A mystery operation has been performed on the first two numbers in each equation to get the third number. Can you figure out what number completes the last equation?

$$5 \star 6 = 10$$
$$3 \star 9 = 7$$
$$4 \star 7 = 8$$
$$5 \star 5 = \underline{\quad}$$

85. Adding the Numbers

$$9 + 8 + 7 + 65 + 4 + 3 + 2 + 1 = 99$$

The above equation uses the digits 9 to 1 and seven plus signs to total 99. Can you use the same digits in the same sequence, using fewer plus signs, and reach the same total of 99? No other mathematical signs may be used.

86. Land for Sale
Regina bought some property for $100,000 and wants to sell it so she'll get a 14% profit. The realtor will want a 5% commission for handling the sale. What should Regina list the property for so she'll make her profit after the realtor gets his percentage?

87. The Years Fly By
Five times what Wyatt's age will be five years from now is 12 less than six times what his age will be six years from now. What is Wyatt's current age?

88. Park Decoration
A workman was placing some decorative plants around a fishpond. The plants were uniform in size and were spaced equally apart. When placing the 14th plant, he noticed that it was directly opposite the first one he'd started with. How many more plants will he need to complete the circle?

89. Pizza Party

A club of 30 high school students contracted with a restaurant to serve pizza and soft drinks for a party that they all attended. One of the students, who excelled in math, remarked that if five fewer of them had shown up it would have cost each $2 more. What was the rate per person?

90. Give Me Five

The number 25 is equal to 5^2. There is one other way to arrive at 25 using the numbers 2 and 5 only once—besides writing the number "25," of course! What is it?

91. The Flower Girl

A girl sold 8 carnations and 6 roses, and received $10. If she had sold 8 roses and 6 carnations, she would have taken in $11. What was the price of the flowers?

92. Math Mistake

TWO × TWO = THREE

Replace the letters with numbers to make this a correct equation. The same letters always represent the same number.

Chapter 3
Word Games

"I respect a man who knows how to spell a word more than one way." —Mark Twain.

93. Fenced In
What do these words have in common?

HEART	IRATE	ACRONYM
KNOWN	LONER	AGAINST
TRAVEL	AMULET	SANDY
APATHY	HIRED	FILLY
CLOSEST	FACTORY	MAGENTA

94. A Bit of the Blarney
Can you decipher the code and read this old Irish toast?

INM LHA KOY NUY ORO WBU SEB YFE OOI URN
AEH RTE EHA DEV EDE AEN DVA.

95. Around the Square
Two ten-letter words can be found in the square below, one reading clockwise and one reading counterclockwise, both skipping every other letter. What are they?

E	A	X	C	P	I
T					E
E					R
U					N
L					A
R	B	E	A	C	D

96. You Can Count on It

longer

teamwork

therefore

flour

effusive

The above words follow a pattern. Can you find a common uncapitalized word that continues the sequence? How long can you keep the sequence going?

97. It's Only Proper

Name four words that change their pronunciation if you capitalize them.

98. Four in a Row

The word "hijack" is spelled with three consecutive letters of the alphabet, as are "inoperative" and "deft." Can you find two common English words (not proper names) that are spelled with four consecutive letters of the alphabet? What if phrases are allowed?

99. Missing Links

Ten nine-letter words have been broken up into three strings of three letters each; then the middle three letters were removed and the other three-letter strings rearranged. Can you match the word beginnings on the left with the correct word endings on the right, and fill in the missing middles to recreate the original ten words? Some beginnings may work with more than one ending (and vice versa), but only one arrangement will allow all the strings to be paired.

CHO	RAE
FOR	OWN
NIG	DAY
WHI	ATE
VER	FUL
SOM	ERY
MAC	OOL
YES	ERE
EXP	IZE
HAR	ION

100. Hidden Word

Q	U	S	L	F
G	O	A	B	Y
R	N	I	M	H
J	T	D	E	K
Z	C	X	W	V

A 14-letter word is hidden in the grid above. It can be found starting in one square (you must figure out which) and moving a square at a time to any horizontally, vertically, or diagonally adjacent square. Letters may only be used once.

101. Another Irish Toast
Replace the letters to decipher the code. Letter substitutions are consistent throughout; that is, if the letter A stood for an M in one place, every A would stand for M.

ZTL ZBNAIECKQW AIDDIJ LIK

CFW EWNC IA LIKE DBAW,

TQV QWOWE PTCPF KU.

102. Time to Rhyme
The nonsense phrases below rhyme with some old sayings. How many can you solve?

1) SPARES SEW POOL MICA COLD TOOL
2) A MANY SHAVED BIZ A JENNY CHURNED
3) THEN THE BATS ALLAY, THE ICE SPILL SPRAY
4) A PITCH IN SLIME PAVES VINE
5) A JEWEL PANNED WHIZ SUNNY FAR MOON STARTED
6) THE BURLY HERD BETS THE GERM
7) A MARKING HOG CLEVER LIGHTS
8) CALL CAT CRITTERS HIS HOT COLD
9) A BOWLING CONE LATHERS THOUGH LOSS
10) WORDS LOVE A WEATHER CLOCK TO HEATHER
11) EVER BOOK A LIFT COARSE IN THE SOUTH
12) FAN CHAPEL AWEIGH REAPS THE PROCTOR ASTRAY
13) DARES BOW CHASE BIKE DOME

103. Upon Reflection ...
What do the following words have in common?

banana	revive
assess	potato
uneven	grammar
voodoo	igniting

104. Spelling Test
Choose the correctly spelled word, A or B.

	A	B
1)	Coolly	Cooly
2)	Supersede	Supercede
3)	Irresistible	Irresistable
4)	Guerilla	Guerrilla
5)	Alright	Allright
6)	Seperate	Separate
7)	Tyranny	Tyrrany
8)	Harrass	Harass
9)	Desiccate	Dessicate
10)	Indispensable	Indispensible
11)	Achieve	Acheive
12)	Nickel	Nickle
13)	Reccomend	Recommend
14)	Desperate	Desparate
15)	Liquify	Liquefy
16)	Dispel	Dispell
17)	Cemetary	Cemetery
18)	Subpoena	Subpena
19)	Definately	Definitely
20)	Embarass	Embarrass

105. The Right Stuff
Replace the letters to decipher a rejoinder for an argument.

EA E MCWLLP XEZQ DTV

XL XTVKP OTZQ OL XWTHC.

106. Don't Look
In a dictionary, which letter of the alphabet has the most pages of words beginning with that letter?

107. Ready for a Walk

What did the motorist say to his car when he looked at his gas gauge? Use only seven letters of the alphabet, each only once and all different.

108. Letters From a Letter

OMICRON is the 15th letter of the Greek alphabet. Can you make 15 or more words of three letters or longer from the letters that spell it? More than 15?

109. Do You Copy?

Which of the words in this series does not fit?

SAME

MEAT

ATTACH

CHARGE

GENTLE

LEAVE

VERBAL

LATEST

110. Let's Ride!
Replace the letters to decipher the famous quotation.

LPZ UQ VE NXPW XPW BGL

UQ VE IZX XPW U IP BSZ

LKKLIUBZ ISLCZ GUNN VZ.

111. A Sad Tale
Farmer John planned to clear a tree stump from his pasture and used a homemade time bomb that would blow up five minutes after he set it. After setting it and moving to a safe distance away, he was dismayed to see his prize bull had entered the pasture and was eating the bomb. How could you describe this situation in one word? Disgusting? Deplorable? Nauseating? Obnoxious? Abominable? Detestable?

There soon followed a loud explosion. What word can describe this tragic tale? Unequivocal? Consummate? Noble? Outrageous? Prodigious?

112. Five-Letter Words
Form a square of five 5-letter words (the same five reading across and down), using 4 A's, 3 D's, 4 E's, 1 G, 4 I's, 3 M's, 1 N, 2 S's, 2 T's, and 1 R. Some have been placed to get you started.

M				M
	N		S	
		G		
	S		D	
M				R

113. Dictionary Definitions

For each of the following words, find a synonym that begins with the letter D.

1) Goal
2) Prevent
3) Merit
4) Loosen
5) Extent
6) Rot
7) Take out
8) Vanquish
9) Sunshine

114. Word Expansions

Take the words below, add the two given letters, and anagram to make new words. How many can you solve?

HERO + G P = _____
PEEN + H W = _____
BERTH + C U = _____
MOOSE + W H = _____
RIDGES + A C = _____
NAPE + T U = _____
TENOR + U F = _____
TIRE + H M = _____
NEIGH + R A = _____
BRUTE + O L = _____

115. Body Parts

SSPTOLKEMAIEDNNCEHY

Three parts of the human body are hidden in the above sequence of letters. Each can be read from left to right (not always in consecutive letters), and each letter is used in exactly one body part. What are they?

116. Before and After
List ten words of six letters or fewer whose first two letters are exactly the same as the last two letters. Example: ONION.

117. Five-Letter Words
How many five-letter words can you make from the letters in the word COMPUTER?

118. Hide and Seek
Can you find nine boy's names hidden in the following sentence?

> "And yet I'm not willing to lend one dollar
> to my greedy uncles."

119. Sound Off
What do the letters of the alphabet B, M, P, and W have in common? What do F and V have in common? And what do the letters D, G, H, J, L, N, and T have in common?

120. A Bad Spell

This page has a word on it that is mispelled. Can you find it?

121. Don't Get Seasick

Reading from the leftmost column to the rightmost column, and using each letter exactly once, make five five-letter words with a nautical flavor.

B	H	A	C	T
Y	U	R	A	S
C	E	L	H	H
G	O	A	R	L
S	A	C	L	K

122. Next!

Can you determine the pattern of the series of numbers below, and figure out what number should come next?

$$80 \qquad 74 \qquad 63 \qquad 53 \qquad ?$$

123. Fussy Eater

Lucy likes walnuts but not peanuts, peas but not carrots, lettuce but not radishes, and tomatoes but not potatoes. Why?

Chapter 4
Challenging Logic Problems

"Logic is the beginning of wisdom but not the end."
—Leonard Nimoy

124. My Own Grandpa
Greg's grandfather is only 9 years older than his father. There was no adoption, divorce, or illegal marriage. Can you explain this situation?

125. Captured by Cannibals
An explorer captured by cannibals was told by the chief that if he guessed how they were going to kill him, he would be boiled alive, and if he guessed wrong, he would have his head chopped off. He made his guess, and the cannibals were forced to set him free. What was his guess?

126. Red Sails in the Sunset
Venice, Florida, is noted for its beautiful sunsets. However, in this town the sun is more than 2,000 miles nearer at noon than it is at sunset. How is this possible?

127. Add Them Up
Rearrange these numbers so that each row of three will add to the same amount horizontal, vertical, or diagonally.

1	2	3
4	5	6
7	8	9

128. Inside Out
I have a T-shirt with a pocket on the left front. Early one morning while dressing in the dark, I put the shirt on inside out, with my left arm in the right sleeve and the right arm in the left sleeve. Would the pocket be on the inside or outside? Front or back? Right or left?

129. Day Daze
What day would the day after tomorrow be if Monday was three days after the day before yesterday?

130. Going to the Movies
There are four adjacent seats left in a movie theatre. Colleen insists on sitting next to Shannon, but refuses to sit next to Sue. If Sue does not sit next to Sean, who is sitting next to Sean?

131. Hog Hassle

A farmer has eight pigs—four brown, three white, and one black. How many can say they are the same color as another pig?

132. How High Is Up?

A student in a physics class devised six different ways to measure the height of a tall building using a barometer. How many can you think of?

133. Present and Accounted For

Gaze at this sentence for just about sixty seconds and then explain what makes it quite different from the average sentence.

134. Time Will Tell

My watch loses 10 minutes each hour. If I set it at noon, what would the correct time be when the watch says the time is 6:00 P.M.?

135. The Bus

In the picture below, in which direction is the bus traveling?

136. Family Reunion

There are two mothers, two fathers, two sons, two daughters, a sister, brother, aunt, uncle, niece, nephew, and cousin at a family reunion. What is the smallest number of people that can be present to represent these relationships?

137. The Test of Strength

Mike, a muscular weightlifter, likes to brag about his strength. George is an office worker whose main physical activity is using a computer keyboard. Tiring of Mike's boasting, George wagers ten dollars that he can push a loaded wheelbarrow for a certain distance and that Mike will not be able to push the same load back. Mike triples the bet as he claims his strength is ten times greater than George's (and it is). Yet George wins the bet. How?

138. Get Your Goat

A goat was put into a fenced-off field that measured 40 feet by 40 feet, with a 20-foot rope tied to his collar. How many square feet of grass could he eat?

139. Cold-Blooded Criminal

Klondike Pete had a large amount of gold nuggets stolen from his cabin in the Yukon. The robbery was discovered during the evening when his neighbor Jake called the police. Jake said he'd noticed a light in Pete's window, which was completely covered with frost, and saw that the front door lock was broken. He went on to tell the police that, since he knew Pete was at the nearby outpost buying supplies, he had sneaked over and scraped enough ice from the frosty window to see what was going on, and saw a big man with a black eye patch wearing a red parka and warming himself at the fireplace in the cabin. The police arrested Jake and found the gold nuggets in his cabin. How did they know he was lying?

140. Shopping for Coffee

While shopping at a local market a thrifty woman found that her family's favorite coffee sold in three different sizes. Size A was 50% more expensive than Size C and contained 20% less weight than Size B, which was 50% heavier than Size C, but cost 25% more than Size A. Which size was the most economical?

141. Selling Candy Bars

Larry and Pat were selling candy bars to raise money for a school trip. Larry had 30 bars priced at two for $1, which would earn $15. Pat had 30 smaller bars priced at three for $1, and would earn $10. However, on the day they were to go door-to-door selling them, Pat was sick. Larry offered to sell Pat's bars as well as his own. To save time he decided to sell the bars at five for $2. He sold all the candy and was dismayed to find that he had only made $24, instead of the expected $25. How is that possible?

142. A Handful
I have a number of coins in my hand. If I added the same number of coins, plus half as many again, plus 2 1/2, I would have 20. How many coins do I have?

143. Tee Totaling
The yardages for the nine holes at the Point o' Woods golf course are 300, 325, 225, 250, 275, 400, 200, 350, and 375. I am in possession of a highly advanced set of ten experimental clubs (designed by pioneers in the field of golf technology) that each shoot the same distance every time, give or take a foot or two, and never slice or hook shots. Club #9 will always cover 50 yards; #8, 75 yards; #7, 100 yards, #6, 125 yards, #5, 150 yards, #4, 175 yards, #3, 200 yards, #2, 225 yards, and #1, 250 yards. (There is also a putter, which invariably sinks any ball within a few feet of the pin.) I have no caddy, and wish to complete the course using only two clubs and the putter. If I chose to use #8 (75 yards) and #6 (125 yards) I could complete the course in 37 strokes (28 approach shots and 9 putts). Back shots are permitted if a shot goes past the green. What clubs must I choose to beat a score of 37?

144. Fishy Story
While on vacation, Charlie bought a fancy fishing pole that was 5 feet, 3 inches long. The airline won't accept any items over 5 feet long, though, and the pole can't be bent or taken apart. How can he bring it home with him on the plane?

145. Underwater Exploration
Fill the empty squares with something found in the sea to make 6 three-letter words reading from top to bottom.

T	E	A	A	P	C
P	E	K	E	N	Y

146. Security Guard

Merchandise was being stolen from a company's warehouse, so the company hired a security guard to observe employees on their way out. Luigi left each night with a wheelbarrow filled with empty cardboard boxes, which the guard always checked very thoroughly, but never found anything inside. After three weeks both Luigi and the guard were fired. Why?

147. Mind Your P's and Q's

Replace the letters with numbers to make the equation correct. The same letters always represent the same number.

$$PDQ - PD = QQ$$

148. Leftovers

I'm thinking of a number. If you divided my number by 4, there would be 1 left over; divide it by 5 and there would be 2 left over; divide it by 6 and the remainder would be 3. The number I'm thinking of is the lowest possible number with these characteristics. What is it?

149. Eight Rings

A jeweler has eight gold rings that look identical, but one is actually gold-plated brass and slightly heavier than the others. How can he determine which one it is by using his balancing scale only two times?

150. Cool Off!

What would the temperature be in Fahrenheit if it was twice as cold as 0°F? (This is not a trick question.)

151. Relatively Confusing

I am having lunch with my only sister's husband's mother-in-law's only daughter-in-law. Who would that be?

152. How Time Flies!
Brian is now twice as old as Rosie was when she was two-thirds as old as she is now. Their combined ages are 91. How old are they?

153. A Weighty Problem
You have three pairs of marbles, one red, one yellow, and the other green. They look identical but one of each pair is slightly heavier than the other. How can you determine which are the heavy ones by using a balancing scale only twice?

154. A Cool Find
An archeologist, while digging in an extremely frigid part of the world, discovered a body that was estimated to have been buried many centuries ago. He claimed that it was Adam, the first man, and was able to prove it. Why does he believe that he can prove it?

155. Brothers and Sisters
In a particular family, each boy has exactly three brothers and each girl has exactly four sisters. How many siblings are in the family?

156. Blackout
It is two days after a major storm and there is a citywide blackout. Street lights and traffic signals are inoperative. An elderly lady dressed in black is trying to cross at an intersection. The road is black, and she is not carrying or wearing any reflectors. A motorist in a sedan with tinted windows, the headlights turned off, and traveling at a normal speed, stops and assists the woman across the intersection. How was he able to see her?

157. Art Thieves, Smart Thieves
Mr. Gotrocks, a very wealthy man, finds that a Van Gogh painting worth two million dollars has been stolen from his mansion. He receives a ransom note from the thieves stating that the painting will be returned if he gives them a $100,000 diamond, which they know he owns. He is to take the diamond at midnight to a certain location on a remote road. Once the stone is authenticated, he will get his painting back. Gotrocks calls the police, who cover every avenue of escape from the meeting place, but who somehow fail to catch the thieves. How did they get away with it?

158. Hidden Connections
What do the things in each row have in common?

1)	fish	delicatessen	piano lesson
2)	comb	shark	saw
3)	needles	hurricanes	potato
4)	coin	kites	dogs

159. Shopping Spree

Christine went on a shopping spree. In the first store she spent half of her money plus $2. In the next store she spent half of what was left plus $1. Her purchases in the third store cost half of what was left plus $1. At the last store she spent half of what was left and had $3 to take home. How much money did she start with?

160. Digital Computing

I'm thinking of a four-digit number in which the first digit is one-third of the second, the third is the sum of the first and second, and the fourth is three times the second. What is it?

161. I've Gotta Split

One of the words below does not belong with the others. Which one?

BEGINNING   PLUMMET   CURTAIL

MODESTY   TAPESTRIES   PROSECUTE

HATRED   FINAGLE   CHARTREUSE

162. Naming Names

A couple named their four children (from oldest to youngest) Mary, Amber, Michelle, and Isabel. They just had another daughter. Which of the following would continue the pattern they've used so far: Julia, Simone, Ruth, Molly, or Elizabeth?

163. Escape

Two reporters were captured by rebel guerrillas in a small war-torn country. They were imprisoned in a tiny courtyard surrounded by a concrete fence which was too high for them to scale. Nobody was guarding them, so they planned an escape. They found an old broken pail and a piece of tin and tried digging under the wall—but the foundation was too deep. Despite this they managed to get away. How?

164. Hunting for Trouble

The proprietor of a hunting store became suspicious of a man who was trying to purchase an exceptionally large amount of ammunition. He called the police, who arrived and questioned the man. He explained he was buying supplies for a target shooting competition and showed the following invitation to prove it:

YOU ARE INVITED

TARGET SHOOTING COMPETITION

DRINKS   BUFFET   DINNER

Where? . . . . Happy Trails Hunting Lodge
When? . . . . Saturday, August 10
Who's invited? . . . . All Your Friends:

Wiley Jane Ted Tom Art Corky Kate Ray Myron Tracy
Grady Trudy Hank Wes Norm Flo Dan Andy Sandy

The sharp-eyed deputy looked at the invitation for several moments and then had the man taken in for intensive questioning. Why did he arrest him?

165. Chicken Show

Frank took 16 crates of chickens to the state fair. He had 24 hens and 12 roosters and exhibited their crates in a square stack, two rows high with three crates on each side, and 11 chickens visible from any side of the stack, as shown below.

Top layer

1	5	1
5	■	5
1	5	1

Bottom layer

1	2	1
2	■	2
1	2	1

After the judging, he returned to pick up the chickens and found that the chickens had been rearranged. He checked the cages and saw that no crates were empty and each side still showed 11. But when he returned home he found that 10 chickens were missing. What happened?

166. Wedding Bells

After many years, Charlie married his childhood sweetheart, Jane. His wife Sarah was one of the bridesmaids. Shortly after the wedding he and Sarah left on a ten-day cruise to Alaska. How can you explain this?

167. Happy Birthdays

Jack was born two hours after his twin sister Jill but celebrates his birthday the day before hers. Why?

168. Happy New Year

New Year's Day is exactly one week after Christmas, so they always fall on the same day. Or do they? Can you think of a year in which they would fall on different days?

169. Please Recycle

Suppose a recycling plant can make 1 new glass bottle from 10 used glass bottles. The bottles produced from these recycled bottles are also recycled. What is the greatest number of bottles that can be made from 5,000 used bottles delivered to the recycling plant?

170. Tic-Tac-Word

In this tic-tac-toe variant, words are printed on cards, and players take turns picking cards until one holds three cards with a common letter. What's the best opening move?

ARMY	CHAT	DISH
GIRL	HORN	JOBS
KNIT	SWAN	VOTE

Chapter 5
Kids' Stuff

"Great changes in the destiny of mankind can be effected only in the minds of little children." —Herbert Read

171. Hold the Ketchup
What is the world's record for eating hamburgers?

172. Heavy Foot
Stand erect, with your hands at your sides. Raise your right foot a few inches up and down. Now press the side of your left foot and your left shoulder against a wall or door frame. Can you raise your right foot now?

173. Kiss the Wall
With your back about two feet from a wall, using your arms for support, can you lean backwards and kiss the wall?

174. Hop the Stick
This is best done outside on a lawn or soft surface, as it's easy to stumble while attempting to do it. Stoop, and with both hands hold a broomstick or 3-foot rod close to the ground in front of you. Without releasing your grip, jump over the broomstick with both feet at same time. Now, while still holding the rod, try to jump backward over it with both feet.

175. Top Heavy?
Face a wall. Place your feet three foot-lengths from the wall. Bend over so that your head touches the wall and fold your hands behind you. Now try to stand erect without moving your feet or hands. Girls can do this easily but boys cannot.

176. Write a 6
While sitting, move your right foot in a clockwise circle. Without stopping, write the number 6 on the palm of your hand.

177. Extra Finger
Place your hands at arm's length in front of you. Make the hands into fists. Now point your index fingers toward each other and bring them together until they touch. While staring at the fingers, slowly bring them toward you. Instead of seeing two index fingers touching, you will see a short finger with a nail at each end held between those fingers. Move your index fingers slightly apart, staring at the center—you will see a "little finger" floating in the middle.

178. How Strong?
Hold your index fingers together, about a foot in front of you. Let a person try to pry them apart by holding your wrists, but keeping their arms straight, and not pushing upward or down, but only pulling sideways.

179. Mind Reader

Here's a magic trick you can do with an assistant. Place nine magazines in rows of three on the floor. Claim your assistant is a mind reader, who can guess which magazine you will choose. Your friend leaves the room, and returns after a magazine is chosen by an audience member. You indicate one of them with a pointer and ask "Is this the one?" The mind reader says, "No, it's ..." and reveals the correct magazine.

The trick is, when you ask "Is this the one?" you touch the pointer to the area of the cover corresponding to the location of the chosen magazine. For instance, if the lower right one was chosen, you'd point to the lower right corner of any other magazine. Touching the upper middle of any magazine would reveal that the correct magazine was the center one in the top row. With practice, you can do the same trick with more magazines, if you're precise about where you place the pointer.

180. Sunset

This is an old fisherman's trick to determine how much time is left before sunset. Face the sun with your hand held at arm's length. Fill the space between the bottom of the sun and the horizon with your fingers. Each finger represents about 15 minutes before sunset, so, for instance, three fingers would mean it was 45 minutes to sunset. After the sun sets completely, there will still be about 30 minutes of light left.

181. Stumped

See if you can read this aloud quickly without stumbling:

A skunk sat on a stump. The stump said the skunk stunk, and the skunk said the stump stunk. The truth is, both the skunk and the stump stunk.

182. Circles

With your arms bent at the elbows and held at chest level make your hands into fists. With thumbs pointing at each other, at the same time, rotate one fist toward your body and the other one away from it.

183. For Multilinguals

The words NI and SAN are Japanese for "two" and "three," TRE is Italian for "three," VIER is German for "four," and CINCO is Spanish for "five." What unusual property do all those words have in common with the English word FOUR?

184. Fraction Action

Can you add up these fractions in your head?

$$\frac{1}{1} + \frac{2}{2} + \frac{1}{2} + \frac{1}{3} + \frac{1}{6} = ?$$

185. Years and Years
Johnny told his teacher that he was nine years old last year, and will be twelve years old next year. His teacher replied that he was right. How is this possible?

186. Black Magic
Here's another mind-reading trick to perform with an assistant. With this trick, your assistant leaves the room and an audience member selects any object in the room. Your assitant returns and you point to objects one at a time until he says, "That's the one!" The secret is, you and your assistant have agreed that when you point to something black, the next item will be the chosen object.

If people think that you've agreed that the fourth (or whatever number) item will be the one, offer to show the trick again, and wait longer to reveal the correct item. You can keep repeating the trick as long as you don't point to the same black item every time. You can also choose another color for your signal, of course.

187. Pop!
Can you stick a pin in an inflated balloon without popping it?

188. The Mighty Straw
Can you penetrate a raw potato with a drinking straw?

189. Not Thirsty
You feed it to keep it alive, but it will die if you give it water. What is it?

190. In Half
Can you fold a piece of paper in half more than seven times?

191. That's Good Eating
A person is told that for five years he can eat as much as he wants, but of one food only. What food should he choose to get the most nutritional value?

192. Mental Mathematics
Add these figures in your mind:

1000 + 40 + 1000 + 30 + 1000 + 20 + 1000 + 10 = ?

193. Free Lunch
Place three coins on a table. Show them to friends and insist that there are four coins there. It is obvious to your friends that there are three coins. Question the friends' eyesight and then ask if they will buy lunch "if there are not four coins there." Of course they will say "yes" and you now tell them that there are indeed not four coins, so they owe you lunch.

194. New Calendar?
Where in the world does February come before January, April before March, July before June, October before September, and December before November?

195. A Good Bet
How can you bet your friends that you can hold your breath for 15 minutes and win?

196. Lucky Seven
If you listed the numbers 1 to 100, how many 7's would you use?

197. Alphabet Soup
What common substance does the letter sequence HIJKLMNO suggest?

198. Doggone It
You have seven dogs. There are huge Labradors and tiny Chihuahuas. You give 5 large biscuits to each of the big dogs, and 4 smaller ones to the Chihuahuas, giving 32 biscuits at a time. How many Labradors do you have?

199. Where There's Smoke
What goes up a chimney down, but not down a chimney up?

200. Free Advice for Gardeners
What is an easy way to determine which of the things growing in your garden are plants or weeds?

201. Mother Knows Best
Jan's mother had three daughters. The first she named April, the second May; what did she name the third one?

202. Giving 110 Percent
I'm thinking of two numbers. One is one and a half times the other, and they add up to 110. What are they?

203. Try It Yourself
What is light as a feather, but the strongest person in the world cannot hold it for more than a few minutes?

204. The Raceway
If a driver can circle a track in 2 minutes and 13 seconds, how long would it take him to make 60 laps? Try to answer without using pencil and paper.

205. A Rose Isn't a Rose
You pay $1 to see a "rose-colored" horse at a carnival sideshow but once inside discover instead a white one eating hay. Can you get your money back?

206. Two Be or Not Two Be
If these ranges of numbers were written out in lists, which would contain the most 2's?

1 to 333   334 to 666   667 to 1000

207. It's Fishy
What kind of fish would chase a mouse?

208. Start Counting
If you counted one number every second for 24 hours a day, approximately how long would it take to count to a billion? A trillion?

209. Adding to Subtract
What can you add to nine to make six? (No, turning it upside down doesn't count as adding something.)

210. Fruity Business
If 4 apples and 6 pears sold for $1.30, and 4 pears and 6 apples sold for $1.20, how many apples can you buy for $1.00?

211. In a Jam
What comes next in this series?

M A M J J ?

Chapter 6
The Good Old Days

212. Do You Remember?

Here's a list of items that you don't see so often nowadays. Divide your age by two, and if you can come up with the correction definitions for that many items, pat yourself on the back for a job well done.

1) Mustard plaster	20) Blotter
2) Muff	21) Humidor
3) Clodhoppers	22) Stoker
4) Bloomers	23) Rumble seat
5) Pompadour	24) Penuche
6) Hoop skirt	25) Running board
7) Cuspidor	26) Watch fob
8) Piano roll	27) Sideboard
9) Hobnail	28) Applejack
10) Damper	29) Pap
11) Bay rum	30) Surrey
12) Coal oil	31) Root cellar
13) Buttonhook	32) Draw plane
14) Cistern	33) Buckboard
15) Stereopticon	34) Haberdashery
16) Bluing	35) Paregoric
17) Whiffletree	36) Box social
18) Lamplighter	37) Bustle
19) Bellyband	38) Trolley pole

Chapter 7
"Impossible" Tricks

"The difficult we do immediately. The impossible takes a little longer." —motto of the U.S. Corps of Engineers

213. Mysterious Coin Trick
Sit at a table. With your arm bent up toward your chin, rest your elbow on the table. Hold a coin in the opposite hand and rub it against the forearm just above the elbow that is resting on the table. During several attempts at rubbing the coin it drops to the table. You pick it up and try again, unsuccessfully, claiming that you probably are not rubbing hard enough. After one last attempt the coin disappears!

214. It Can't Be Done
Think of any number between 1 and 1,000. Do not tell anyone what number you chose, but keep it in your mind and concentrate on it. I claim that I will guess the number, either exactly or plus or minus 1. I write my guess on a notepad, return the pencil to you, and assure all present that nothing is in my hands, hidden up a sleeve, or concealed in my clothes. You now make known the number you chose, and I reveal what is written on the pad. It is the number you picked!

215. Reading the Impossible
Pick a number with 3 different digits. Reverse the number and subtract the smaller number from the higher number. I ask you for only the last digit of your answer and hand you a dictionary, asking you to turn to the page that corresponds with that number. I then tell you the first word on that page. How do I do it?

216. Losing My Marbles

Put two marbles in a bottle and insert a cork in the neck. How can you remove the marbles without removing the cork or damaging the bottle in any way?

217. Coin Con

While out with a group of friends, I ask one of them to mark a half dollar coin without showing it to me and place it face down in his or her open hand. I ask someone else in the group to count to three, after which the first person is to make a fist and keep it tightly closed. I claim that I can make the coin disappear from my friend's fist from across the room. After the count is done, I complain that whoever counted to three did it too fast. (If he or she counted slowly, I complain that the count was so slow that it threw me off.) After a short argument, I say that I will attempt to finish the trick anyway, and ask my friend to open his or her hand. Instead of the half dollar there is a dime, a much smaller coin. I take a half dollar from my pocket and ask them to identify it. Of course, it is the marked coin. How did I do it?

Answers

1. Nations of the World
There are many countries that will work with most letters of the alphabet, but here is one set: Argentina, Brazil, Chile, Denmark, Egypt, Finland, Germany, Holland, India, Japan, Kenya, Luxembourg, Macedonia, Norway, Oman, Philippines, Qatar, Russia, Spain, Turkey, United States, Vietnam, Western Sahara, Yemen, Zambia.

2. Incredible!
In 1998 Ben Lecomte swam the Atlantic Ocean from Hyannis, Massachusetts, to Quiseron, France (3,736 miles) in about 80 days.

3. Oldest Thing Alive?
Bacteria found in the Carlsbad Caverns in New Mexico were analyzed by scientists and estimated to be 250 million years old! They were revitalized in a laboratory after a suspended animation in a shelled spore.

4. Past the Expiration Date
Beer. The earliest known chemical evidence dates it at about 3500–3100 B.C. This time frame surpasses mead, a honey-based wine.

5. Better Make That an Extra Large
Tea.

6. Including You and Me
Everything in the universe is moving, taking up space, and getting older.

7. Fish Story
At Knight's Key, Florida, in June 1912, Charles Thompson caught a whale shark weighing 26,534 pounds (12,036 kg). It measured 38 feet (11.6 m) around and 18 feet (5.5 m) long. (Note that while a whale is a mammal, a whale shark is a fish.)

8. Let's Shrink the Sun
1) Earth's diameter would be approximately 1 inch.
2) The diameter of Mars would be slightly more than half an inch.
3) The distance from Earth to the Sun would be approximately 1,046 feet.
4) The distance from Earth to the Moon would be approximately 32 inches.
5) The nearest star to the Sun is Proxima Centauri; the distance between them would be approximately 53,872 miles.

9. The Birth of Broadcasting
At a Coast Guard station in Massachusetts on December 24, 1913, an unscheduled broadcast was transmitted on a Marconi telegraph network. A homemade microphone was used to air the Christmas story and a selection was played on a violin.

10. City Dwellers
From the latest reports the five most populated cities are:
1. Tokyo, Japan (pop. 28,025,000).
2. Mexico City, Mexico (pop. 18,131,000)
3. Mumbai, India (pop. 18,042,000)
4. São Paulo, Brazil (pop. 17,711,000)
5. New York City, U.S.A. (pop. 16,626,000)

11. Drink Up
It is possible, and Peter Dowdeswell of Earlsbarton, Northamptonshire, U.K., holds the world record for it. He drank 4 pints of beer upside down in 22.1 seconds, and later claimed another record by drinking a gallon of beer in 8 minutes while hanging upside down.

12. Mystery Destination
The Eiffel Tower in Paris, France.

13. Capital Cities
Buenos Aires, Argentina; Canberra, Australia; Vienna, Australia; Brussels, Belgium; Sarajevo, Bosnia; Brasilia, Brazil; Ottawa, Canada; Beijing, China; Havana, Cuba; Copenhagen, Denmark; Cairo, Egypt; Helsinki, Finland; Paris, France; Berlin, Germany; Athens, Greece; New Delhi, India; Rome, Italy; Dublin, Ireland; Tokyo, Japan; Vaduz, Liechtenstein; Mexico City, Mexico; Amsterdam, Netherlands; Oslo, Norway; Manila, Philippines; Warsaw, Poland; Moscow, Russia; Singapore, Singapore; Bern, Switzerland; Washington, D.C., United States; London, United Kingdom; Caracas, Venezuela; Hanoi, Vietnam.

14. Hole to China
The surface of the earth is 70% water. The chance of finding land directly opposite land is very slight, only about 1%. Opposite the United States is the Indian Ocean. The only diametrical land would be a tiny island in line with a small town in Iowa. A few miles of coastline of Portugal and also the northern tip of South America have land opposite them.

15. Answer When Ready
Fire.

16. Silent and Unseen
Radio waves.

17. Span-tastic!
The highest bridge in the world was constructed in 2004. It is called the Millau Viaduct, on route A75 in France. It is about 1.5 miles long (2.4 km) and 1,125 feet high (343 m) at its tallest point.

18. Extremes
The hottest temperature was 136°F, in El Acizia, Libya. (A close contender: 134°F, in Death Valley, U.S.) The coldest was −129°F in Vostok, Antarctica.

19. Not So Tough
They all had ailurophobia; that is, they were afraid of cats.

20. What Time Is It?
Floral City, 12 noon Monday; Buenos Aires, 1 P.M. Monday; Denver, 10 A.M. Monday; Tokyo, 2 A.M. Tuesday; Siena, 6 P.M. Monday; Moscow, 8 P.M. Monday; Jefferson City, 11 A.M. Monday; Hong Kong, 1 A.M. Tuesday; Sydney, 3 A.M. Tuesday; Stockton, 9 A.M. Monday; Wexford, 5 P.M. Monday; Bangalore, 10 P.M. Monday.

21. High Rise
The four tallest building structures in the world are:
Taipei 101, Taiwan, 1,671 feet (509 m)
Petronas Twin Tower 1, Kuala Lumpur, 1,483 ft. (452 m)
Petronas Twin Tower 2, Kuala Lumpur, 1,483 ft. (452 m)
Sears Tower, Chicago, U.S., 1,451 ft. (442 m)
The skyscraper Burj Dubai is now under construction in United Arab Emirates and expected to be completed in 2009. It will be 2,313 feet (705 m) high, and will be the tallest man-made structure of any kind in the history of the world.

22. Eight Is Enough?

N is next; they are the initial letters of the names of the planets in our solar system. Until recently, P would have followed N, but Pluto was reclassified as a dwarf planet in 2006, along with Eris and Ceres.

23. Not Out of the Woods Yet

The tallest tree in the world, located in a redwood forest in California, is 379.1 feet tall (115.54 m). Its exact location is kept secret because the last record-tall tree was destroyed by vandals.

24. Around the World

Belgium, Netherlands, France, Germany, Poland, Russia, Mongolia, China, and Canada.

25. Between the Oceans

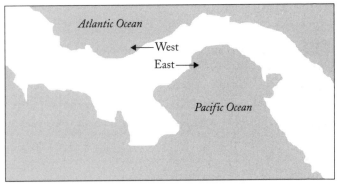

In the Panama Canal Zone, part of the eastern shoreline is on the Pacific Ocean and part of the western coast is on the Atlantic Ocean.

26. Let's Travel

China, Israel, Sudan, Italy, Algeria, Germany, Nepal, Serbia, Denmark, Niger, Laos, Suriname, Tonga, Peru, East Timor, Eritrea, Iran, San Marino.

27. Moving In
It is estimated that only 28% of Africa is undeveloped. (The United States is 38% undeveloped.)

28. Thank You
1-i, 2-k, 3-j, 4-l, 5-a, 6-h, 7-b, 8-f, 9-c, 10-e, 11-g, 12-d.

29. Move Over
They each span two continents. (Europe and Asia, except Egypt, which is mostly in Africa and partly in Asia.)

30. A Trip to the Winery
Ten miles. We would be back where we started because all the directions were "turn left," and all the distances traveled between turns were equal.

31. Good Friends
Canada and the United States.

32. Older Than a Buzzard
Albatross (43 years), cockatoo (75 years), and parrot (up to 100 years).

33. Drive On
The Pan-American Highway, which is 24,140 kilometers, or about 15,000 miles. It extends from Fairbanks, Alaska, to Brasilia, Brazil.

34. Almost the Most
Europe. (Asia is the most populated.)

35. Seafood Diners
Japan, with a population of over 100 million, has the largest seafood consumption in the world. The people of Japan eat seafood almost daily.

36. Hole Notes

The deepest hole dug by human hands (and shovels and pickaxes) is known as "The Big Hole," and was started in 1870 when diamonds were discovered in the town of Kimberley, South Africa. It is 2.4 kilometers deep (over 7,000 feet). The Kola Peninsula in northwestern Russia has the undisputed deepest hole in the world. It is over 7 miles (about 11 km) deep. It is a bore hole made to study the Earth's core.

37. Astronomical?

Two times two equals four no matter how many times you multiply it.

38. The Flagpole

24 feet.

39. Highway Travelers

Both would be the same distance from Fairbanks when they met on the highway.

40. Half Fun!

63.

41. Big Business

Nathan made a $2 profit on the transactions.

42. Sitting Ducks

It would take seven days for three ducks to lay three eggs, and seven days for fifteen ducks to lay fifteen eggs. Each duck lays just one egg per week.

43. Clock Watcher

1, 2, 3, 4, 5, 6, 10, 11, 8, 9, 12, 7 is one possible arrangement.

44. Over and Under
14.

45. Dividing It Up
Megan $4,000, Maggie $1,000, Lauren $1,250.

46. No Adding
$11 \times 11 - (1 \div .1) - 11 = 100$
$2 \times 2 \times 2 \times 2 - (2 \div 2) - 2 - 2 = 11$
$3 \div .3 \times 3! - 3^3 = 33$
$(44 \div 4 - (4 \div .4)) \times 44 = 44$
$5! - (5.5 \times 5) - 5.5 = 87$
$666 \times .6 - 66.6 = 333$
$(777 - (77 \times 7)) \div 7 - 7 = 27$
$888 \div .888 \times .8 = 800$
$(99 - 9) \div 9 \times (99 \div 9) - (9 \div .9) - (9 \div 9) = 99$

47. Ignorance of the Lawn Is No Excuse
The fifth lap, which is 33 1/3 feet past the halfway point.

48. I Think That I Shall Never See ...
The tree grows 1.5 feet per year.

49. Traveler's Check
$4 \times 1963 = 7852$

50. Seating the Guests
$1 \times 2 \times 3 \times 4 \times 5 \times 6 \times 7 \times 8 \times 9 \times 10 \times 11 \times 12 = 479,001,160$
different ways to seat the guests.

51. Cops and Robbers
The police would have caught the robbers after driving 10 more miles, traveling 30 miles in 30 minutes compared to the robbers' 30 miles in 40 minutes.

52. Dividing the Loot
The total amount was $22,000. The leader took $12,000, the second thief got $6,000, and the driver got $4,000.

53. Missing Number
16. Divide the first two numbers in each row by 3 and 2 respectively; the two answers added together equal the third number.

54. Computerization
Lauren contributed $85, Maggie gave $95, and their father paid $945.

55. Cash Customer
$45 and a bottle of wine.

56. Drive to the Airport
The airport is 100 miles away, and I usually drive at 50 miles per hour.

57. Plus and Minus
$0 + 1 + 2 - 3 - 4 + 5 + 6 - 7 - 8 + 9 = 1$. Other solutions are possible.

58. Square Deal

1	15	14	4
12	6	7	9
8	10	11	5
13	3	2	16

59. Good Hunting
The dog ran .9 of a mile.

60. Football Practice
Nine throws. The first throw was 15 feet and the last throw was 27 feet.

61. Those Mighty Nines
$99 \div 9 - (9 \div 9) = 10$
$99 \div 99 + 9 = 10$
$9 + (9 \div 9) \times (9 \div 9) = 10$
$9 + 9 - 9 + (9 \div 9) = 10$
$9 \div (9 \div 9) + (9 \div 9) = 10$
(Other solutions are possible.)

62. Buying Rope
He ordered 9 feet and 2 inches but got 2 feet and 9 inches.

63. Division of Labor
2,520 is the lowest number that can be divided evenly by any number from 1 to 10.

64. Quick, What's the Answer?
Half of 2 is 1, and 1 plus 2 equals 3.

65. Chicken Shopping
17 roosters ($34), 5 hens ($25), and 78 Chicks ($39).

66. Clearance Sale
The 30-meter and 36-meter rolls were sold on the first day, and the 32-meter, 38-meter, and 62-meter rolls were sold on the second day. The 40-meter roll was left over.

67. Eight Training
If the last three digits of any number are divisible by 8, the number will always be divisible by 8. We can see that the last three digits of 127,677,981,804 aren't divisible by 8 (being 4 more than 800), so that's the odd one out.

68. Four You Alone

$1 = (4 \div 4) \times (4 \div 4)$
$2 = (4 \div 4) + (4 \div 4)$
$3 = (4 + 4 + 4) \div 4$
$4 = (4! - 4 - 4) \div 4$
$5 = (4 \times 4 + 4) \div 4$
$6 = (.4 \times 4) + 4.4$
$7 = 44 \div 4 - 4$
$8 = (4 \times 4) - (4 + 4)$
$9 = (4 \div 4) + (4 + 4)$
$10 = (44 - 4) \div 4$

Other solutions are possible.

69. Cookie Time

120 cookies. 40 + 30 + 24 + 20 = 114, with 6 left over.

70. Sharing the Profits

The cook got $2,516; the waitress, $2,214; the busboy, $1,634; and the dishwasher, $1,556.

71. Words From Numbers

S L A N G	S A L A D
L O W E R	A B A C I
A W A R E	L A T I N
N E R V E	A C I N G
G R E E K	D I N G Y

72. The Calculating Jogger

The man has three-quarters left of the bridge to cross, which would take 2 minutes, 15 seconds. After 2 minutes, he'd be 15 seconds from the end. The train will reach the bridge after 1 minute, and then in another minute travel the distance it takes him 2 minutes, 45 seconds to run, catching him. Therefore 8 mph times 2.75 (two and three-quarters minutes) equals the train's speed times 1, and the train's speed is 22 mph.

73. The Race
Rachel would win. Let's say that the track is 1 mile, and each is capable of running a mile in 6 minutes. Katie will cover half the distance in 3 minutes and the other half in 6 minutes, finishing the race in 9 minutes. If Rachel runs the same amount of time that she walks, the distance she runs will be twice the distance she walks, so she'll run two-thirds of the race in 4 minutes, and walk one-third in 4 minutes, finishing in 8 minutes, 1 minute faster than Katie.

74. Squared Numbers
$3^2 + 7^2 + 9^2 = 139$
$2^2 + 3^2 + 4^2 + 5^2 + 6^2 + 7^2 = 139$

75. Bus Riders
The bus left the terminal with 12 women and 14 men.

76. Presents of Mind
Each grandson receives $24. One grandson gets two red envelopes (each with a $5 bill), four blue envelopes ($3), and two green envelopes ($1). The other two grandsons each receive three red envelopes ($5), two blue envelopes ($3), and three green envelopes ($1).

77. Exchanging Change
He has 12 dimes and 6 quarters, making $2.70. If he had 6 dimes and 12 quarters, he would have $3.60.

78. Driving to Work
It's impossible to make up the time; I've already driven the amount of time it normally takes me to get to the office.

79. Weight Watcher
Joe weighs 125 pounds and Sue weighs 10 pounds (she's a baby).

80. Halves and Quarters
400.

81. Hours of Fun
$6 \div (5 \div 4 - 1) = 24$
$4 \div (1 - (5 \div 6)) = 24$

82. Math Teaser

2	+	0	+	7	= 9
×		×		−	
6	÷	3	×	5	= 10
÷		+		÷	
4	×	8	−	1	= 31
= 3		= 8		= 2	

83. Three Ways
49 and 56. (There are other ways to fulfill the condition, but this is the one that uses the smallest amount of candy.)

84. Test Yourself
The number 5 completes the last equation. The number on the right of each equation is equal to the product of the two numbers on the left minus 20.

85. Adding the Numbers
$9 + 8 + 7 + 6 + 5 + 43 + 21 = 99$

86. Land for Sale
The property should list for $120,000, a figure reached by dividing the cost plus profit by 95, then multiplying by 100. The realtor will receive $6,000, leaving $114,000 (the cost plus $14,000).

87. The Years Fly By
Wyatt is 1 year old.

88. Park Decoration
It would take 12 more to complete the circle, making 26 plants total.

89. Pizza Party
The party cost $300, which cost the club members $10 per person. If there had been 25 partygoers instead of 30, they would have had to pay $12 apiece.

90. Give Me Five
$5 \div .2 = 25$

91. The Flower Girl
Roses cost $1, and carnations cost 50 cents.

92. Math Mistake
$138 \times 138 = 19,044$

93. Fenced In
Removing the first and last letters of each word leaves another word.

94. A Bit of the Blarney
The toast reads "May you be in heaven an hour before the devil knows you are dead." To decode the message, read the last letter of every group of three letters in order, then the second letters of every group of three, then the first letters.

95. Around the Square
"Expendable" and "caricature."

96. You Can Count on It

The names of the numbers one to five can be read from left to right in the words (though not in a consecutive sequence of letters). The next word could be "sphinx" or "transfix," both of which contain "six" from left to right. Our longest sequence goes to eleven, with "subservient," "eyesight," "nickname," "tavern," and "selectiveness" (you may find other words that also work). There's no single word that we know of that contains "twelve" in nonconsecutive letters.

97. It's Only Proper

Polish (the nationality) and polish (as in furniture polish), Ares (the god) and ares (the metric units of area), Job (the biblical character) and job (as in an occupation), Reading (the city) and reading (the activity). There are others as well: August (the month) and august (meaning "dignified") can also have different pronunciations, as can Mobile (the city) and mobile (the adjective); and Lima (the city) is pronounced differently from the "lima" in "lima beans." Count yourself right if you thought of any four, and congratulations if you thought of any we missed.

98. Four in a Row

"Understudy" and "overstuffed" are two common words that contain the sequence RSTU. There is also the less common word "gymnoplast" (MNOP), and, if you allow phrases, "film noir" (MNOP) and "public defender" (CDEF), among others.

99. Missing Links

CHOCOLATE   SOMEWHERE
FORGETFUL   MACHINERY
NIGHTGOWN   YESTERDAY
WHIRLPOOL   EXPULSION
VERTEBRAE   HARMONIZE

100. Hidden Word
Ambidextrously

101. Another Irish Toast
May misfortune follow you the rest of your life, and never catch up.

102. Time to Rhyme
1) There's no fool like an old fool.
2) A penny saved is a penny earned.
3) When the cat's away, the mice will play.
4) A stitch in time saves nine.
5) A fool and his money are soon parted.
6) The early bird gets the worm.
7) A barking dog never bites.
8) All that glitters is not gold.
9) A rolling stone gathers no moss.
10) Birds of a feather flock together.
11) Never look a gift horse in the mouth.
12) An apple a day keeps the doctor away.
13) There's no place like home.

103. Upon Reflection ...
If you delete the first letter of each word, what's left is a palindrome.

104. Spelling Test
1-A, 2-A, 3-A, 4-B, 5-A, 6-B, 7-A, 8-B, 9-A, 10-A, 11-A, 12-A, 13-B, 14-A, 15-B, 16-A, 17-B, 18-A, 19-B, 20-B.

105. The Right Stuff
"If I agreed with you we would both be wrong."

106. Don't Look
The letter S.

107. Ready for a Walk
OICURMT. ("Oh, I see you are empty!")

108. Letters From a Letter
Twenty that we found are: moronic, micron, croon, minor, coin, corn, icon, iron, mono, moon, morn, norm, room, con, coo, ion, moo, nor, rim, roc. Others are possible.

109. Do You Copy?
The last two letters of each word are the first two of the next word. LATEST breaks the pattern.

110. Let's Ride!
One if by land and two if by sea and I on the opposite shore will be. (From Henry Wadsworth Longfellow's "The Ride of Paul Revere")

111. A Sad Tale
Abominable (a bomb in a bull) and noble (no bull).

112. Five Letter Words

M	A	D	A	M
A	N	I	S	E
D	I	G	I	T
A	S	I	D	E
M	E	T	E	R

113. Dictionary Definitions

1) Destination
2) Deter
3) Deserve
4) Detach
5) Degree
6) Decay
7) Delete
8) Defeat
9) Daylight

114. Word Expansions
Gopher, nephew, butcher, somehow, disgrace, peanut, fortune, hermit, hearing, trouble.

115. Body Parts
Stomach, spleen, kidney.

116. Before and After
Decide, honcho, emblem, salsa, orator, iconic, tomato, church, edited, shush. (Many more answers are possible.)

117. Five-Letter Words
We found 23 common to fairly common words: comer, comet, coupe, court, crept, croup, cruet, cuter, erupt, metro, moper, outer, outre, recto, recut, repot, route, tempo, toper, trope, truce, trump, tumor. How did you do?

118. Hide and Seek
Andy, Tim, Will, Len, Don, Ned, Art, Tom, Reed, and Les.

119. Sound Off
B, M, P, and W cannot be pronounced without closing your lips. F and V require touching the top teeth to the lower lip. D, G, H, J, L, N, and T can be pronounced only by touching the tip of your tongue to the roof of your mouth.

120. A Bad Spell
Mispelled is misspelled.

121. Don't Get Seasick
In alphabetical order, the words are BEACH, CORAL, GULLS, SHARK, and YACHT.

122. Next!

43. To get the next number in the series, subtract the amount of letters in the previous number from that number. For example, "eighty" has 6 letters, so the number after 80 is 80 − 6 = 74.

123. Fussy Eater

She likes foods that grow above the ground, rather than underground.

124. My Own Grandpa

Greg's father is older than Greg's mother, and the statement refers to Greg's maternal grandfather. If Greg's grandfather was 19 when Greg's mother was born, and Greg's father and mother were 30 and 20, respectively, then Greg's father and maternal grandfather would be 30 and 39 at his birth.

125. Captured by Cannibals

He replied that they would chop his head off. Since they couldn't kill him without creating a contradiction, he was set free.

126. Red Sails in the Sunset

The sun is always farther away from any given point on Earth at sunset than it is at noon. This would be true not only in Venice but anywhere on the planet.

127. Add Them Up

2	7	6
9	5	1
4	3	8

128. Inside Out
The pocket would be on the inside, on the left, in the back. Now don't forget to put the shirt back on the right way around before you go outside!

129. Day Daze
Tuesday.

130. Going to the Movies
Colleen. They would sit: Sean, Colleen, Shannon, Sue.

131. Hog Hassle
Let's hope you didn't fall for this one. Pigs can't talk.

132. How High Is Up?
1) Use the barometer to measure the air pressure on the roof of building and on the ground, then convert the difference in millibars (units of atmospheric pressure) to feet to give the height of the building.

2) Take a barometer to the roof, drop it over the edge, and measure the time it takes to reach the ground. Taking into account acceleration due to gravity, this can be used to determine the distance fallen.

3) Measure the barometer, then climb up or down the fire escape on the outside of the building, marking barometer measurements on the wall as you go. Count the number of marks on the wall to find the height of the building.

4) When the sun is shining, measure the length of the barometer and its shadow, compare it with the shadow of the building, and use the proportions to determine the height of the building.

5) Tie the barometer to a string, lower it to the ground from the roof, and then measure the string.

6) Offer to give the barometer to the janitor if he'll tell you the height of the building.

133. Present and Accounted For
The sentence contains all the letters of the alphabet.

134. Time Will Tell
If the watch takes an hour to run 50 minutes, it takes six minutes to run five, so an hour on the watch is equal to an hour and twelve minutes. At 6:00 on the watch, the correct time would be 7:12.

135. The Bus
The answer depends on what country you're in. The door (which we can't see in the picture, so must be on the opposite side of the bus) opens on the curb side of the bus. In countries where vehicles are driven on the right side of the road, the bus would be going from right to left on the page. In countries where vehicles are driven on the left, the bus would be moving from left to right on the page.

136. Family Reunion
Four. A sister and a brother, one with a son (who has a child, not at the reunion), and the other with a daughter (who also has a child, not at the reunion).

137. The Test of Strength
George tells Mike to get in the wheelbarrow and pushes him.

138. Get Your Goat
He was able to graze the whole pasture (1,600 square feet), because the rope was not tied to a stake.

139. Cold-Blooded Criminal
The police knew Jake was lying when he said that he scraped the ice from the outside of the window. Because of the heat from the fireplace, the frost would have formed on the inside of the window.

140. Shopping for Coffee
Size C is the best buy. Size A and Size B are equal in value; both cost 25% more per unit weight than Size C.

141. Selling Candy Bars
Larry's pricing would work if every sale included 2 large bars and 3 small bars. After 10 sales, however, all the small bars would be sold, leaving 10 large bars, priced at 40 cents each (five for $2) instead of 50 cents each (two for $1). Therefore he lost 10 cents each on the last 10 large candy bars, coming out $1 short in the end.

142. A Handful
Seven coins.

143. Tee Totaling
The course can be completed in 35 strokes (26 approach shots and 9 putts) with the putter and clubs #7 (100 yards) and #6 (125 yards). The approach shots for each hole are: $300 = 3 \times 100$, $325 = (2 \times 100) + 125$, $225 = 100 + 125$, $250 = 2 \times 125$, $275 = (3 \times 125) - 100$ (back shot needed), $400 = 4 \times 100$, $200 = 2 \times 100$, $350 = (2 \times 125) + 100$, $375 = 3 \times 125$.

144. Fishy Story
He found a shallow cardboard box measuring 15 inches by 5 feet, put the pole in it diagonally and closed the box. It passed the 5-foot regulation.

145. Underwater Exploration
Oyster.

146. Security Guard
Luigi was stealing wheelbarrows.

147. Mind Your P's and Q's
109 – 10 = 99

148. Leftovers
The number is 57.

149. Eight Rings
Weigh three rings against three rings. If they balance, the heavy one is one of the other two. Weigh those two to see which is heavier. If one of the sets of three rings is heavier, take two of them and weigh them to see if one is heavier. If they balance, the unweighed one of the three is the ring you are looking for.

150. Cool Off!
The question is "What would the temperature be if it was twice as cold as 0°F?" The answer depends on the meaning of the phrase "twice as cold." Any answer depends on the reference unit of temperature and the zero point of that temperature. The significance of zero degrees Fahrenheit is arbitrary; zero degrees Celsius is the freezing point of water. The most relevant temperature scale is Kelvin, the thermodynamic temperature scale. Zero degrees Kelvin is "absolute zero," the point at which all molecular activity ceases. There is no temperature colder than absolute zero; therefore, it is the best reference point to use when answering this question. The formula to convert Fahrenheit to Kelvin is:
$$K = (F - 32) \times {}^{5}/_{9} + 273.15$$
Using this formula, we find that zero degrees Fahrenheit is equal to 255.4 degrees Kelvin. Half that (or twice as cold as that) is 127.7 degrees Kelvin. We convert that back to Fahrenheit with this formula:
$$F = (K - 273.15) \times {}^{9}/_{5} + 32$$
This equals –229.8 degrees Fahrenheit, which is our answer.

151. Relatively Confusing
My wife.

152. How Time Flies!
Rosie is 39 and Brian is 52.

153. A Weighty Problem
Let us identify the six marbles as R1, R2, Y1, Y2, G1, G2. First, weigh R1 and G1 against Y1 and G2. If that weighing balances, weigh G1 against G2. If G1 is heavier, then R2, Y1, and G1 are the heavy marbles. If G2 is heavier, R1, Y2, and G2 are the heavy marbles.

If the first weighing was uneven, the green marble on the heavy side of the scale is the heavier of the green marbles. Next, weigh R1 and Y1 on the left against G1 and G2 on the right. Let's say R1 and G1 outweighed Y1 and G2 in weighing 1. G1 is heavy, and there are three possibilities for R1 and Y1: (a) R1 heavy, Y1 heavy; (b) R1 heavy, Y1 light; and (c) R1 light, Y1 light. (It can't be R1 light and Y1 heavy, or the first weighing would have balanced.) If the left side is heavier, it's (a); if the scale balances, it's (b); and if the green marbles are heavier, it's (c). If the right side of the scale was heavier on the first weighing, G2 is heavy, and the same three possibilities for the second weighing apply, except that (b) is R1 light, Y1 heavy.

154. A Cool Find
The body did not have a navel.

155. Brothers and Sisters
Nine children (four boys and five girls).

156. Blackout
It was daytime.

157. Art Thieves, Smart Thieves

When Mr. Gotrocks reached the location he found a small remote-controlled helicopter. He placed the diamond inside, and the police were unable to follow it as it flew off. The painting was returned the next day.

158. Hidden Connections

1) They all have scales.
2) They all have teeth.
3) They all have eyes.
4) They all have tails.

159. Shopping Spree

She started with $64.

160. Digital Computing

1,349.

161. I've Gotta Split

Finagle. The other eight words can all be split up into two shorter words: BEG + INNING, PLUM + MET, CUR + TAIL, MODE + STY, TAPES + TRIES, PROSE + CUTE, HAT + RED, CHART + REUSE.

162. Naming Names

Simone. Names begin and end with the second and the second-to-last letter of the preceding name. Hopefully their next child will be a son, so they can name him Ivan.

163. Escape

They used the metal and pail to scoop dirt against one corner of the wall. When the pile was high enough they could reach the top of the wall by climbing up the pile of dirt, and thus escape over the wall.

164. Hunting for Trouble

The deputy read the list of names invited, and found a hidden message starting with the first letter of the list of invited names, and reading every third letter. The message reads, "We attack armory at dawn Monday."

165. Chicken Show

A clever chicken thief rearranged the chickens in the crates so that the same number would be visible from each side of the stack, even with ten chickens missing. Here's how the thief did it:

Top layer

3	1	4
1		1
4	1	3

Bottom layer

1	1	1
1		1
1	1	1

166. Wedding Bells

Charlie was a minister who performed the wedding ceremony for Jane and her husband.

167. Happy Birthdays

The parents were on a boat from China to America. Jill was born on Tuesday, they crossed the International Date Line, and Jack was born on Monday.

168. Happy New Year
They fall on different days every year. New Year's Day is on January 1, and Christmas is December 25, almost 12 months later, on a different day of the week.

169. Please Recycle
The plant can make 555 bottles: 500 from the 5,000 to start with, 50 from those 500, and 5 from those 50.

170. Tic-Tac-Word
Rearrange the words so that the words in each row, column, and long diagonal share one letter:

SWAN	JOBS	DISH
ARMY	HORN	GIRL
CHAT	VOTE	KNIT

The center square is the best opening play in tic-tac-toe, so HORN, the word in the center, is the word to choose.

171. Hold the Ketchup
The record is 103 burgers in 8 minutes, at the World Hamburger Eating Championship in Knoxville, Tennessee.

183. For Multilinguals
Each of these words is spelled with the same number of letters as the numbers they represent: NI = 2, SAN = 3, etc.

184. Fraction Action
The total is 3.

185. Years and Years
Last year he was 9 years old until his birthday, when he turned 10. This year he'll turn (or has already turned) 11, and next year he'll turn 12.

187. Pop!
Inflate the balloon, then put a piece of transparent tape on the spot where you will stick the pin into the balloon (or multiple pieces of tape, if you want to use more than one pin). This will prevent it from popping. From a few feet away the tape cannot be seen, so this makes a good stage trick.

188. The Mighty Straw
Cover one end of a plastic drinking straw with your thumb so the air can't escape and strike the other end into the raw potato.

189. Not Thirsty
Fire

190. In Half
No matter how large the sheet of paper is, it cannot be folded in half more than seven times.

191. That's Good Eating
This may surprise you, but pizza is said to be a food with just about all of the nutritional values required for a balanced diet.

192. Mental Mathematics.
4,100. (Many people incorrectly say 5,000.)

194. New Calendar?
In the dictionary, where the months of the year are listed alphabetically.

195. A Good Bet
Blow into a balloon, tie it, and hold in your hand for 15 minutes.

196. Lucky Sevens
20 (Did you remember to count all the 7's in the 70's?)

197. Alphabet Soup
H to O suggests water, or H_2O.

198. Doggone It
Four Labradors and three Chihuahuas.

199. Where There's Smoke
An umbrella.

200. Free Advice for Gardeners
Simply pull out everything, and anything that comes up again is a weed.

201. Mother Knows Best
Jan.

202. Giving 110 Percent
44 and 66.

203. Try It Yourself
Breath (unless you use a balloon).

204. The Raceway
2 hours and 13 minutes. (1 minute multiplied by 60 is an hour, and 1 second multiplied by 60 is a minute.)

205. A Rose Isn't a Rose
"No, you can't have your money back! Haven't you ever seen a white rose?"

206. Two Be or Not Two Be
The range 1 to 333 would have the most 2's.

207. It's Fishy
Fish don't chase mice—not even catfish.

208. Start Counting
It would take about 32 years to count to a billion, and 31,689 years to get to a trillion.

209. Adding to Subtract
Add S to the Roman numeral IX and you get SIX.

210. Fruity Business
You can buy 10 apples for $1.00. (Pears cost 15 cents.)

211. In a Jam
A, for August; the letters are months, starting with March.

212. Do You Remember?
1) Mustard plaster: Counterirritant for chest colds
2) Muff: Fur piece to keep hands warm
3) Clodhoppers: Work shoes
4) Bloomers: Women's undergarment
5) Pompadour: Hairdo with the hair brushed up high
6) Hoop skirt: Skirt with a bell-like shape
7) Cuspidor: Pot used to spit in
8) Piano roll: Roll of punched paper used to control player pianos
9) Hobnail: Nail used to fasten heels to shoes
10) Damper: Device in chimney to control draft
11) Bay rum: Aftershave lotion
12) Coal oil: Fuel for lamps
13) Buttonhook: A hook for pulling buttons through buttonholes
14) Cistern: Tank for storing rain water in cellars
15) Stereopticon: A projector with two lanterns that fades from one image to the next

16) Bluing: Liquid used in laundering to whiten clothes
17) Whiffletree: Crossbar for a draft animal's harness
18) Lamplighter: Someone hired to light gas street lamps
19) Bellyband: Strap around a draft animal's body
20) Blotter: Absorbent sheet used to dry ink
21) Humidor: Small box to keep cigars fresh
22) Stoker: Person who adds fuel to furnaces or boilers
23) Rumble seat: Open-air seat in the rear of a coupe
24) Penuche: Candy made of brown sugar, milk, nuts, and butter
25) Running board: Step to assist passengers entering or leaving a car.
26) Watch fob: Chain that connects a watch to a vest pocket
27) Sideboard: Chest used to store silverware and linens in a dining room
28) Applejack: Alcoholic drink made from fermented cider
29) Pap: Milk thickened with flour and sugar, fed to infants in Depression days
30) Surrey: Horse-drawn carriage with two or four seats
31) Root cellar: Underground storage chamber for fruits and vegetables
32) Draw plane: Knife with two handles, used to plane wood
33) Buckboard: Open four-wheeled horse carriage
34) Haberdashery: A store selling men's clothing and accessories
35) Paregoric: Opium-based painkiller
36) Box social: Fund-raiser in which people bid on box lunches and the privilege of dining with the person who prepared the purchased meal
37) Bustle: Underskirt padding for women's clothes
38) Trolley pole: Pole repositioned by the conductor at the end of a trolley to allow the trolley to run in the opposite direction

213. Mysterious Coin Trick

The arm on which you rub the coin is bent up so your hand touches your chin. When you drop the coin use that hand to it pick up, then transfer it to the other hand. On the last attempt you pick up the coin and pretend to put it in your other hand. Instead, drop the coin into a shirt pocket or into your collar while all eyes are on your rubbing hand. Always practice first.

214. It Can't Be Done

Use a quarter-inch piece of soft lead such as that found in a No. 1 pencil. (No. 2 pencils write too lightly.) Cut a tiny piece of transparent tape or flesh colored adhesive bandage. With about half of the lead exposed, tape it to the pad of your thumb, about half an inch from the tip of the thumb. Now practice writing with that thumb while holding the pad on your lap. Merely pretend to write on the pad when the person is concentrating on the number. Return the pencil, and place the pad face down. Reveal to all that your hands are empty, with fingers spread slightly, palms down and flipped over and back rather quickly, keeping the lead out of sight. Also assure that there is nothing up your sleeves or in your pockets. Pick up the pad, and when the number is recited to you (dramatically ask for it to be repeated if you need more time), write that number with your thumb which is concealed by the pad. Divert attention from the pad by not looking at it while writing, and by talking about how you learned this skill from a Tibetan monk or some other such distracting patter. If you perform the trick multiple times, you should sometimes deliberately write a number that differs by one from the correct number, to confuse the audience, who won't suspect that you'd be wrong on purpose. Patience and practice are needed to do this trick.

215. Reading the Impossible

No matter what number is picked, when reversed and subtracted, the remainder will be either 99, 198, 297, 396, 495, 594, 693, 792, or 891. (Notice that the first and last digits always total nine—if you imagine that the first digit of 99 is a zero—and the middle digit will always be 9.) This trick requires some advance work. Since I know which ten numbers are possible answers, I memorize the first word on those ten pages of my dictionary. If I had performed this trick in your home, I would have had to find your dictionary first and memorize quickly.

216. Losing My Marbles

Push the cork inside the bottle and remove the marbles.

217. Coin Con

My friend with the coin is a secret confederate. We have previously agreed what mark will be made on the half dollar. The dime is concealed in the crook of his or her thumb so it cannot be seen while the palm is open. When I complain loudly about the count, I divert the group's attention for the split-second we need to accomplish our prank. The marked coin is dropped into his or her other hand and the small coin falls into place.